monday morning®

SUPER CIRCLE TIME
SUMMER

by Patty Claycomb

Publisher: Roberta Suid
Production: Little Acorn & Associates, Inc.

SUPER CIRCLE TIME SUMMER
Entire contents copyright © 2004
by Monday Morning Books, Inc.

For a complete catalog, write to the address below:
Monday Morning Books, Inc.
PO Box 1134
Inverness, CA 94937

Call our toll-free number: 1-800-255-6049
E-mail us at: MMBooks@aol.com
Visit our Web site:
http://www.mondaymorningbooks.com

ISBN 1-57612-203-4

Printed in the United States of America
9 8 7 6 5 4 3 2 1

Contents

Introduction

Summer has a mystique all it's own. The word 'summer' conjures up images of warmth, long days, time off, blue skies, green grass, and a myriad of summer activities. As a teacher, this can be a time to keep minds and hands occupied in fun and inexpensive ways. Summer experiences can involve creative water and sand play, relaxing in lawn chairs, playing with beach balls, and washing objects outside with buckets and sponges. This is truly a season to get sandy, muddy, and wet. A preschoolers dream!

Summer is a great time to introduce children to the outside environment and what happens when the air is warm. Observe the growth of buds and flowers. Observe green hills and leafy trees. Look down for ant hills and up for bird nests. And listen! What summer sounds do you hear? Do you hear mowers, ice cream trucks, or the sounds of people walking and talking? Summer brings you outside more than any other season!

And one more thing. This is a great time to talk about the sun! The sun is what allows us to experience all the wonderful parts of summer. Introducing the sun can be done in an easy to understand way. The sun is yellow. The sun is up in the sky. The sun is round. The sun gives us warmth. The sun is a star!

Summer is definitely a time to slow down, take deep breaths, and take a closer look at the world. Enjoy the warmth on your skin. Do sun dances. Find dandelions. Blow fuzzy weeds and make wishes.

Summer is: Warm–Yellow–Water–Sand–Relaxing–Daydreaming–Popsicles!

Things to talk about:

1. Ask questions about sounds. "Is the sun making a sound?" Sit very still and try to listen. The summer sun warms us, but you can't hear it.

2. During the summer, you might hear sounds of people doing things in warm weather. What kind of sounds might you hear? Brainstorm! Possible sounds might be: a skateboarder, a roller-skater, an ice-cream truck, a radio, the sound of a jogger, a child playing, a lawn mower, birds chirping and people walking and talking.

3. Let some sounds in. Open a window. Now sit very still. What sounds can you hear?

4. You can identify things by their sounds. Ask everyone to close their eyes. When you tap someone on the shoulder, this child can say, "Hello!" Can you identify who the child is by the sound of his or her voice?

Materials: None

Preparation: None

Things to do:

1. Explain that you will say a word. For example, say the word, "bees." Ask everyone what sound bees make. They buzz!

2. Now say "bees." The children answer by saying "buzz!" Practice a few times.

3. Explain that you will name things that make sounds in the summer. The children will fill in the sound. Possible examples are:

Bees (buzz)	Hummingbirds (hum)	Skateboards (rumble)
Birds (chirp)	Lawn mowers (roar)	Ice-cream trucks (play songs)
Ducks (quack)	Children in pools (splash)	Dogs (bark)

4. After you have said these words and sounds, repeat them. See who can remember the responses.

More Ideas:

• Go on a Sound Walk. List the sounds you hear on a poster board. Add photos of things you saw that made the sounds.

Sun Dancing

Things to talk about:

1. Ask the question: "Who would like to do an experiment?" Explain that music makes people do something. What does music make us do? Brainstorm!
2. Play some music. Have everyone sit and observe what happens. Notice that music makes you move.
3. Why do people dance to music? Possible answers might be: It is good exercise; Some people dance because it is their job; Some people dance for fun; Some people dance to celebrate something.

Materials:

Yellow and orange crepe paper, yarn, colored construction paper, tape, felt pens, scissors

Preparation:

Cut the crepe paper and yarn into strings. Cut strips of paper to fit around a child's head.

Things to do:

1. Celebrate the sun and warm weather with a Sun Dance. Make your costumes from material suggested above.
2. Make headbands. Everyone can choose a colored paper strip and draw designs.
3. Children can then tape strings of yarn and crepe paper around their headband. Now tape the headbands around each child's head.
4. Children can add to their costume by tying yarn and crepe paper streamers on their wrists, arms and legs.
5. Now go outside. Play recorded music. Dance to celebrate the sun.

More Ideas:

- Add shakers and tambourines.
- Draw a large circle with yellow chalk. Everyone can dance inside the sun.

Yellow Ball Relay

Things to talk about:

1. Sit in a circle. Show a yellow ball. Ask the question: "How am I holding this ball?" Brainstorm! A possible answer is: With your fingers.
2. Look at your fingers. Bend them. Wiggle them. Open and close them. Explain that fingers can do many things. One thing they can do is hold objects.
3. Pass the ball around the circle. Have everyone observe how their fingers are curved around the ball.
4. Now hold the ball. Explain that if you relax your muscles, the ball will drop. Demonstrate.
5. Give everyone a turn to hold the ball and then relax their muscles.

Materials:

A yellow ball

Preparation: None

Things to do:

Pretend the ball is the summer sun. Brainstorm a variety of ways to pass the "sun," around your circle. Try them out. Listed below are possible ways to pass the ball:

- Pass the ball slow. Pass it fast!
- Use only one hand to roll the ball around the circle.
- Pass the ball behind your backs.
- Bend your knees. Pass the ball under the bridges.
- Close your eyes and pass the ball.
- Sit on your knees and use your head.

More Ideas:

- Play music while you pass the ball.
- Try standing up and kicking the ball around the circle.

Sun Power

Things to talk about:

Do the activity below. Then place your painted summer sun on the rug. Sit around your sun and brainstorm.

1. Where is the sun? What color is the sun? It is a yellow star.
2. Why is the sun so much bigger than all the other stars in the sky? It is the closest star to our earth.
3. Is the sun hot or cold? The heat, from the sun, warms our earth and warms us.
4. What else does the sun do for us? It gives us light. Look outside the windows. You can see everything because there is light from the sun.
5. Is it light or dark at night? Why is it dark? The sun is not shining on us.

Materials:

Butcher paper, yellow paint, brushes, scissors

Preparation:

Cut a large circle from butcher paper.

Things to do:

1. Place the large paper circle on a table.
2. Provide paint and brushes. Everyone can help paint a summer sun.
3. When the sun has dried, place it on the rug. Sit around your sun. Brainstorm answers to the possible questions listed above.
4. End the discussion with the following question: "What might you feel like doing if you sit in the sun for a long time?" Possible answers might be: Find shade; Drink something cool; Fan yourself.

More Ideas:

- Children can each paint a paper plate yellow and take their own summer sun home.
- Spread out sheets or blankets on the grass. Children can relax in the sun.
- Have children find pictures in magazines that show activities to do on a warm sunny day. Cut them out and tape them on your sun.

The Suntan Lotion Song

Things to talk about:

1. Ask the question: "How can the sun be harmful?" Brainstorm! Possible answers: You can feel sick if you get too hot; If you look at the sun, it can hurt your eyes; If you are in the sun too long, it can burn your skin.

2. How can we protect our skin from the rays of the sun? We can cover our skin with clothing. We can sit in the shade. We can use suntan lotion that prevents our skin from burning.

3. What part of our body do we put suntan lotion on? All parts that are exposed to the sun. Each child can name a body part, such as "elbow," and then pretend to rub on suntan lotion on that body part.

Materials: None

Preparation: None

Things to do:

Sing the following song to the tune of BINGO! Clap as you sing it. When you sing the words itchy and scratch, scratch your skin. After you sing the last verse, carefully touch different parts of your body and yell, "Ow!"

I ran outside to play-O, and sunny was the day-O,
S-U-N-N-Y, S-U-N-N-Y, S-U-N-N-Y
And sunny was the day-O!

I heard my mother yell to me, "Rub on suntan lotion,"
S-U-N-N-Y, S-U-N-N-Y, S-U-N-N-Y,
And sunny was the day-O!

I ran outside to play-O, and did not take my lotion,
Itchy, itchy, scratch, scratch, scratch,
Itchy, itchy, scratch, scratch, scratch,
Itchy, itchy, scratch, scratch, scratch,
And sunny was the day-O!

Sun Spots

Things to talk about:

1. Would you feel the warmth of the sun if clouds covered the sky? Why not? Would you feel the sun if you stood under a large tree? Why not?
2. When would you feel the warmth of the sun? When the sun shines directly on you. Do you like that feeling? How does it make you feel?
3. Some people are sun people. They love being in the sun. Is anyone here a sun person?
4. What do you think sun people like to do in the sun? Brainstorm! Possible answers are: Lie out in the sun; Go walking or hiking in the sun; Read in the sun; Go swimming; Ride a bicycle; Ride in a convertible!
5. If you woke up on a sunny day, what is one thing that you would like to do?

Materials:

Yellow posterboard or construction paper, scissors, a pen

Preparation:

Cut a circle from yellow paper. This is a sun spot. Make a sun spot for each child.

Things to do:

1. Give a sun spot to each child. Pretend that the sun spots represent the warmth of the sun. Place them between your palms. Imagine the warmth of the sun and how it feels.
2. Now look around the classroom. Are there places where the sun is warming the room? Are there places that feel more warm than other places?
3. Children can walk around the classroom and feel for warm spots. These spots might be near windows or places near the walls.
4. When you find a warm spot, place your sun spot on it.
5. Observe the classroom. Look how the sun warms our room.

More Ideas:

• Take your sun spots outside. Place your sun spots on places that feel very warm.
• Draw pictures on your sun spots. Draw something that you like to do in the sun.

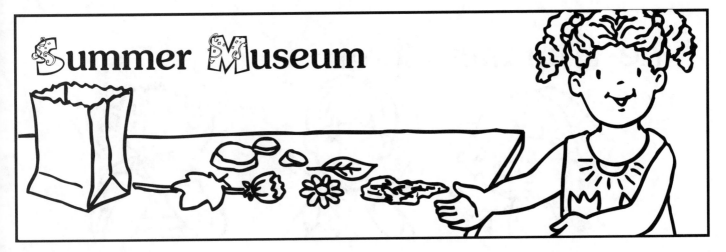

Summer Museum

Things to talk about:

1. What is a museum? It is a place you can visit where you learn about things. A museum displays many collections. You can go and see these things and read information about them on signs.
2. If you saw a stuffed grizzly bear at a museum, what do you think the sign might say? It might tell you about its height, weight, coloring, what it eats and where it lives.
3. You can find almost anything in a museum. What would you find? Brainstorm! Possible answers might be: sea animals, insects, rocks, seashells, a moon rock, very old pottery, jewelry, and art. You might even find the skeleton of a Tyrannosaurus Rex.
4. Who would like to visit a museum? If you could visit a museum, what would you like to see there?

Materials:
Long sheets of colored construction paper, small paper bags, a felt pen

Preparation:
Print each child's name on a sheet of construction paper.

Things to do:

1. Create a summer museum. Give each child a paper bag. Print the children's names on their paper bags.
2. Go outside with your paper bags. Look for summer treasure that you want in your museum. Examples of treasures might be: rocks, leaves, twigs, flowers, or a piece of bark.
3. Everyone can place their own finds in their paper bags.
4. Each child can display their treasures on sheets of paper. Encourage the children to arrange their treasures in a way that pleases them.
5. Place the sheets of summer treasures in a row.
6. Play museum! Pretend to give a guided tour of your Summer Museum. Observe and talk about the objects on each child's paper.

More Ideas:
• Advertise the opening of your Summer Museum. Offer tours to parents or any visitors in the classroom.

The Summer Chant

Things to talk about:

1. Ask the question: "What is a song?" Brainstorm! A song has words. You sing a song. Sing a short song together.
2. What is a chant? You say a chant! Provide an example. Say together: "One, two, buckle my shoe!"
3. Explain that songs and chants have rhythm. Listen for rhythms. Clap to the tune of *Jack Be Nimble*. Clap as you count from one to ten.
4. Say a child's name. Clap the name! For example, if the name is Jennifer, clap three times, on each syllable. Clap each child's name.

Materials:

Butcher paper, tape, scissors, a black marker

Preparation:

Cut a large sheet of butcher paper. Tape it low on a wall. Print the word "Summer" on the paper.

Things to do:

1. Clap the two syllables in the word "summer." Clap them slow. Clap them fast.
2. Now learn *The Summer Chant*. Below are suggested body movements.

   For the first line: Clap fast for the words "sweet-sweet." Then clap once for "summer." For the words, sizzling at last, put hands in the air, wiggle fingers and move hands downward.

   For the second line: Pretend to strum. Strum a fast two beats for the words "green-green."
   For the third line: Raise a fist in the air twice.
   For the fourth line: Shake your fist.
   For the fifth line: Fan yourself.
   For the sixth line: Move arms like you are swimming.

> ### The Summer Chant
>
> Sweet-sweet summer is sizzling at last!
> Play the ukulele in the green-green grass.
> Mama! Mama!
> Can you make me a shake?
> Then tell me I can cool off,
> In the cool-cool lake

More Ideas:

• Try this chant slowly, along with the body movement. Try it fast.
• Draw a picture of the chant. Tape a large sheet of butcher paper on the wall. Draw grass.

Baby Bird Boogie

Things to talk about:

1. Why do you think mother birds lay eggs in warm weather? Brainstorm! Possible answers are: It's nicer weather to sit on an egg; The nest she builds is more strong and stable; When her babies hatch, they will feel warm; It might be easier for the mother bird to find food.
2. Why do you think many bird nests are built in a bowl shape? It helps to keep the baby birds from falling out.
3. When do you think a baby bird leaves its nest? When it is old enough. When it is strong enough. When it has enough feathers to fly with. When the mother bird stops feeding it.

Materials:

Yarn, scissors

Preparation:

Cut a string of yarn long enough to form a large circle. Place the yarn in a circle on the rug.

Thing to do:

1. Sing "The Boogie Song" (next page) and dance to the tune of *The Hokey Pokey*. Stand around the outside of the circle. This is your bird nest. Pretend you are baby birds. Mama bird is off looking for food. You are exercising your bird bodies to make them strong.
2. When your finish the song, jump into the circle. You are now safe inside your nest. Snuggle down and wait for mom.

The Boogie Song

Put your right wing in,
Put your right wing out,
Put your right wing in,
And shake it all about,
Do the boogie woogie,
And flap yourself around,
That's what it's all about!

Put your left wing in,
Put your left wing out,
Put your left wing in,
And shake it all about,
Do the boogie woogie,
And flap yourself around,
That's what it's all about!

Put your right foot in,
Put your right foot out,
Put your right foot in,
And shake it all about,
Do the boogie woogie,
And flap yourself around,
That's what it's all about!

Put your beak in,
Put your beak out,
Put your beak in,
And snap it all about,
Do the boogie woogie,
And flap yourself around,
That's what it's all about!

Put your tail in,
Put your tail out,
Put your tail in,
And shake it all about,
Do the boogie woogie,
And flap yourself around,
That's what it's all about!

More Ideas:

• Sing *The Boogie Song* and use parts of different animals. You can use fins, teeth, jaw, and tail for sharks.

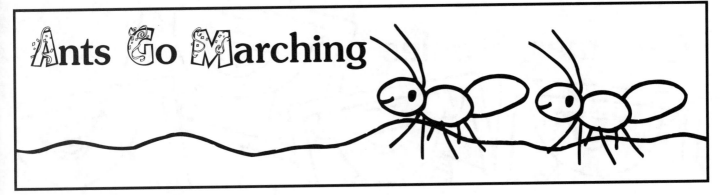

Ants Go Marching

Things to talk about:

1. Who has seen an ant? Can you describe an ant? Where do you think ants live? They live all over the world.
2. If you were an ant, what kind of nest would you build? Brainstorm! Ants build underground nests. Why is this a good idea for a small insect?
3. Ants have different jobs in their ant colonies. What kind of jobs do you think ants have? Some ants look for food. Some guard the nest. Some take care of the eggs. Some grow gardens. One ant is the queen. She lays all the eggs.
4. How can you tell if you know somebody? You remember them by sight. You recognize their voice. Try an experiment. Have a child stand behind another child and speak. Can this child be identified? How does an ant tell if he or she knows another ant? By scent.
5. Ants are strong. They can carry objects fifty times heavier than they are. Could an ant carry a caterpillar back to its nest? Many ants can. They drag it or carry it together.

Materials:

Black construction paper, scissors, yarn, pipe cleaners, one for each child

Preparation:

Cut out an oval to make an ant. Make at least two ants for each child. Cut a string of yarn, ten inches long.

Things to do:

1. Place the yarn on the rug and shape it into a circle. Sit around the yarn. This is the opening to an ant nest. Place an ant by the opening to guard the nest.
2. Give each child an ant. Explain that ants leave scent trails when they walk. They follow each other in a line to look for food.
3. Choose a child to place one ant on the rug. Each child, in turn, can place an ant behind the next ant in line. Count the ants. How many ants have left the nest to look for food? Take turns starting the ant line.
4. Children can place their ants in front of them. Give each child a pipe cleaner. This is a caterpillar. Try to balance the caterpillar on the back of the two ants. Slowly move the ants toward the nest opening.

More Ideas:

- Hide all the ants in the classroom. The children can try to find them. As they find the ants, they can quickly go back to the rug and place them all in a straight line.

Summer Smiles

Things to talk about:

1. Ask the following question: Who knows how to smile? Let everyone demonstrate.
2. Why do you smile? Brainstorm! Possible answers are: When you feel happy; When you are excited; When you see a friend; When you want someone to know you are friendly.
3. How are smiles different? Some people have very large smiles. Some smiles are tiny. Some people show their teeth when they smile. Some people smile with their lips closed. Some people have a crooked smile. Try to show all the different smiles.
4. Invite the children to share what makes them smile. A birthday party? A puppy?

Materials:

Ruler, tape measure, camera, magazines

Preparation: None

Things to do:

1. Invite everyone to share their smiles. Comment on the type of smile they have. Give every smile applause.
2. With a ruler or tape measure, measure everyone's smile. Make a smile chart. Print the child's name and the length of their smile.
3. Take photos of everyone's face, from the nose down. As an option, have these pictures enlarged at a photo store. Place them on a wall or posterboard. Make a sign that reads: Match the child to the smile.
4. Make a smile collage. Cut out smiling faces from magazines. Tape them on a posterboard.
5. Learn *The Smile Chant*. You can clap, or hold a smile drawn on paper. Hold it upside down for most of the song. Turn your frown into a smile on the word, quickly.

> ## The Smile Chant
>
> If you chance to meet a frown,
> Do not let it stay.
> Quickly turn it upside down,
> And smile that frown away!

More Ideas:

- Make smiles for snacks. Cut an apple into wedges. Spread peanut butter along the apple wedge. Add small marshmallows for teeth. If you have a tooth missing, leave a gap.

Sizzling Sun Quilt

Things to talk about:

1. Ask the following questions: "What is a blanket?" "Does anyone have a blanket?" "Is your blanket on your bed?" "What does it look like?"
2. What is a quilt? It covers you like a blanket. It is often handmade. It is made of many squares that are sewn together.
3. What could be inside each square? Patterns or pictures. Everyone can think of pictures or designs that would look pretty on a quilt.
4. If you had a quilt, what colors would it be? Brainstorm!

Materials:

White construction paper, scissors, red, yellow, gold and orange crayons and markers, a hole punch, yarn

Preparation:

Cut the white paper into square shapes. Make one for each child. Cut strings of yarn, long enough to tie the papers together.

Things to do:

1. Explain that everyone can help make a sun quilt. Pass out a square paper to each child. Place the crayons and markers on the rug.
2. Have everyone draw and color in a picture of the sun.
3. When everyone has finished, the children can share their pictures.
4. Collect the sun pictures. Tie them together with the yarn.
5. Hang the sun quilt on a wall. Sit by it. Observe any patterns you might see. Can you find your drawing of the sun?
6. How does the quilt make you feel? Warm? Tired? Do you want to curl up under it and take a nap? Do you want to run outside and play in the sun?

More Ideas:

- Instead of tying the quilt together, you can tape it together with colored masking tape.
- Make a quilt to represent a variety of topics that you study. Make a flower quilt or a face quilt.

The Hot Colors!

Things to talk about:

1. A color can make you feel a certain way. People have favorite colors, because that color makes them feel good or happy. Does anyone have a favorite color? Brainstorm!

2. Some colors make you feel cool. Blue and gray are cool colors. Why would blue make you feel cool or even cold. Answers might be: Blue is the color of ocean water; Ocean water can be cold; A blue whale lives in the ocean; Blue can be the color of your skin, if your body gets really cold.

3. What would be a warm or hot color? Yellow, red or orange. Why are these considered hot colors? They represent things that are hot. Ask for examples. Answers might be: The sun is yellow; Fire is yellow and orange; The tip of a match is red; Lava is red; Hot peppers are red.

4. Look at your clothes. Who has a cool color on? Who is wearing a hot color?

Materials: None

Preparation: None

Things to do:

1. Divide the class according to colors. Have children wearing warm colors sit together. The children wearing cool colors can sit opposite them.

2. Make a hot bridge. The children wearing more hot colors can form two lines, facing each other. The children facing each other can hold hands, high in the air. The cool children can walk through the hot bridge.

3. Make a cool bridge. Do the same as above, to form a cool bridge to walk through.

4. Celebrate the warm colors of summer. Look around the room. Observe warm or hot colors that you see.

5. On the count of three, have everybody stand by a hot color.

More Ideas:

• Use food coloring to make red, yellow and orange ice cubes. Place them on paper plates and watch them melt.

Summer Acrobatics

Things to talk about:

1. Think of ways you can move your body. Brainstorm! As each child comments, do the movement. For example: Move your shoulders up and down; Stand and bend at the waist; March in place; Balance on one foot.

2. Demonstrate how you can do a movement that represents an animal. For example: You can sit on your hind legs and jump. Have everyone guess what you are. A frog. Ask if anyone can do a movement that represents an animal.

3. Do a body movement that represents something that is not an animal. For example: Sit on your legs; Bend your body forward until your head touches the rug; Tuck your arms into your sides. Ask everyone to guess what you are. Give clues. "I am very hard. I am found everywhere. I am often gray. If you are barefoot, and you step on me, you might hurt your foot. I am a rock."

4. Ask if anyone can use their body to represent something that is not an animal.

Materials: None

Preparation: None

Things to do:

Do body movements that represent things you might see in warm weather. Below are possible ideas:

	• **Be a flying fish.** Stand on one leg. Slowly lift your remaining leg behind you, keeping it straight. Continue this movement until your leg is parallel to the floor. Spread arms out for balance. Stand this way as long as you can.
	• **Move as slow as a snail.** Get on your hands and knees. Try to move so slow that you can hardly detect movement.
	• **Be a butterfly,** newly hatched, and drying its wings in the sun. Stand up. Spread out both arms. Don't move.

• **Be a roly-poly bug.** Get on your hands and knees. Walk in place. Then roll into a tight ball.

 • **Be a stork.** Stand on both feet. Slowly lift one leg and bend it at the knee. Balance as long as you can.

 • **Be ocean water,** by the beach, representing the tide. Stand straight. Slowly lean forward. Then slowly lean backwards. Lean both ways as far as you can, without falling over.

 • **Move like a snake**. Lay on your stomach. Tuck your arms against your side. Try to move forward, using only your body muscles.

 • **Be a summer thunderstorm.** Slap the rug, back and forth, with your hands. This is your rainstorm. Clap your hands for thunder and yell boom.

 • **Be a summer rainbow.** Get on your hands and knees. Now slowly raise your legs and move your hands forward on the rug. Make an arch with your body.

 • **Be a group caterpillar.** Form a line on your hands and knees. Follow the head of the caterpillar around the room.

 • **Be a beach ball.** Curl up in a ball. Roll back and forth.

 • **Be a sand crab.** Sit on the rug. Place your hands behind you, palms down. Lift up with your arms and legs. Try to walk forward, with your bottom off the ground.

More Ideas:

• Make a copy of the idea strips on pages 19 and 20 and cut apart. Place them in a jar. Everyone can choose a strip of paper. Read the idea for a body movement. Ask the child if he or she can think of a way to move to match the idea.

One Man Band

Things to talk about:

1. Ask the question: "What do you think the words "one man band" means?" There is one person in the band.
2. One person can play many instruments. Think of instruments you might play in a one man band. Possible answers are: a harmonica, a flute, a banjo, a horn, maracas, bells, and a drum.
3. Some people make sounds, in a band, with their bodies. Think of different ways to make sounds, using just you. You might clap hands, stomp feet, whistle, slap your thighs, and smack your lips together.
4. Give everyone a turn to make a sound, using their body.

Materials: None

Preparation: None

Things to do:

1. Celebrate summer with a "one man band." Learn the movements listed below and sounds.
2. Practice the movements. Do them slowly at first. Gradually increase your speed.
3. Begin by saying the following words. Clap as you say them:

> Summertime, summertime,
> Hot sun.
> Summertime, summertime,
> Have some fun.

4. Now begin your "one man band." Make the following sounds and movements.

- Puff your cheeks out and hit them four times.
- Snap twice.
- Hit your stomach three times, quickly.
- Hit each hip, once.
- Slap thighs twice, at the same time.
- Stomp your feet four times, quickly.
- Clap twice.

More Ideas:

- Everyone can create the "one man band." Each child can think of a movement.

Puzzle Possibilities!

Things to talk about:

1. Who can describe what a puzzle is? Brainstorm! Possible answers might be: Something you put together; A picture broken up into many pieces; Something you solve; Small pieces that fit together to form one large piece.
2. Who has put together a puzzle? How did you do it? What was hard about it? Why was it easy?
3. What are some tricks about putting together puzzles? Answers might be: Look at the picture on the box; Observe the parts; Try to match colors and shapes; Begin at a corner.

Materials:

A calendar, envelopes, one for each child

Preparation:

Tear out calendar pictures, one for each child. With a pen, divide each calendar picture into four, five, or six pieces. Cut these pieces out. Place each cut-up picture into separate envelopes.

Things to do:

1. Give everyone an envelope. Have everyone take out their puzzle pieces. Everyone can piece their puzzles together to make their individual pictures.
2. Draw a vertical line down the center of each calendar picture. Then draw a horizontal line across each picture. Pass out a picture and scissors to each child. Everyone can cut their picture into fourths. Then everyone can mix their pieces up and make their own puzzle.
3. Tape a large sheet of butcher paper low on a wall. Color in a scene. Each child can take a turn and add to the picture. Draw and color a flower garden, fish in a bowl or a swarm of butterflies. Divide the picture into large squares, one for each child. Cut them out. Give everyone a piece to hold. Rebuild the picture on the rug.
4. Divide the children into three or four teams. Place a puzzle in front of each team. Then mix their puzzle pieces up. On the count of three, each team can try to rebuild their puzzle first.
5. Print each child's name on a long strip of paper. Cut out the letters in the names and place each name puzzle in a separate envelope. Each child can get their name envelope and try to build their name.

More Ideas:

• Do a puzzle calendar to match your topics of study. Cut up an ocean calendar when you study the ocean.

Summer Charades

Things to talk about:
1. Talk about the word charades. What do you think it means?
2. Demonstrate. Act out an animal. See who can guess what animal you are mimicking. Charades describes something with body movements, without words.
3. Think of things that you have seen people do, but without words. Possible ideas are: Brush teeth; comb hair; drink a glass of water; jog; type, sleep.
4. What is everyone doing right now? You are sitting and listening.

Materials:
A container, paper, a pen, scissors, a yellow crayon, tape

Preparation:
Cut out strips of paper. Print a summer charade on each strip. Fold them in half and place them in the container. Draw a sun and color it yellow. Tape it on the front of the container.

Things to do:
1. Explain that each charade will start with the word summer. Choose a child to pick a summer charade from the container. This child can act out the charade idea. Offer help if necessary. You can be a part of the charade.
2. For example, you can act out a scene. For summer camp, you can put up a tent, make a fire and roast a marshmallow.
3. Below are summer charade ideas:

• Summer sun	• Summer sunbathing	• Summer soccer
• Summer clothes	• Summer vacation	• Summer garden
• Summer picnic	• Summer rainstorm	• Summer honeybee
• Summer barbecue	• Summer surfer	• Summer mosquito
• Summer camp		

More Ideas:
• Do a summer sports charade, such as, sailing, surfing, water-skiing, badminton and golf.

Things to talk about:

1. Why is exercise important? It builds muscle. It keeps your bones strong. It keeps your heart healthy.
2. Have everyone hold an arm out straight, palms up. Slowly bend the arm at the elbow. Why is your arm able to bend? You have muscle under your skin. Your muscles are strong and they help to move your bones in different positions.
3. Think of ways you can move your arms and legs. Brainstorm! Possible answers are: running, jumping, skipping, swimming, crawling, throwing, catching and standing up.

Materials: None

Preparation: None

Things to do:

1. Sit in a large circle. Choose a child to be "the sun runner."
2. This child stands up and enters the circle. Then he or she can begin to run.
3. The sun runner runs along the inside of the circle. As this child runs, everyone claps their hands and sings the following song to the tune of *Skip, Skip, Skip to My Lou*.

> Run, run, run in the sun,
> Run, run, run in the sun,
> Run, run, run in the sun,
> Run in the sun all day.

4. When you finish the song, the sun runner can choose a child to run in the circle and be the next sun runner.
5. When everyone has been a sun runner, stand up. Hold hands and form a large circle. Celebrate the sun and your strong, healthy bodies. Yell together: "Hip, hip, hooray!" As you say hooray, bring your arms high in the air. Do three yells.

More Ideas:

• Have each child, who stands, do a different movement inside the circle. You can ask the children to skip, tiptoe or crawl. Replace with the word "run" for the matching movement.

Things to talk about:

1. Who has been on a picnic? Where were you? Why do you think people enjoy picnics?
2. What happens on a picnic? Brainstorm! Possible answers are: You eat outside; You sit on a blanket; You bring food in a picnic basket; You relax; You might play games, such as, Frisbee; You might attract ants.
3. If you could bring one type of food on a picnic, what would it be?
4. What can you bring, on a picnic, to protect yourself from the sun? You can wear a hat. You can put on suntan lotion. You can wear sunglasses. You can sit in the shade.

Materials:

A picnic basket, paper plates, a blanket, and plastic or real food. Add food items, such as, ketchup, barbecue sauce, mustard, olives, and potato chips

Preparation:

Place the food and plates in the basket.

Things to do:

1. Spread out a blanket on the rug. Sit in a circle on the blanket.
2. Place the picnic basket in the middle of the circle. Now relax. Yawn. Stretch. Lay down. Close your eyes. Don't get up until the teacher says: Time to eat.
3. Now sit up. The teacher can chose a child to open up the basket. This child can look inside and take out an item of food.
4. This child can now hold up the item and identify it. If it is an apple, the child can say, "Who wants to eat an apple?" The child can then give the apple to a child who is raising a hand.
5. The child who gets the apple can now chose from the picnic basket.
6. Continue until every child has an item of food on their plate.

More Ideas:

- Choose a child to sit by the picnic basket. Blindfold the child. Hand the child an item from the basket. The child can try to guess what it is.
- Make your own picnic baskets. Everyone can bring in a shoe box. Paint them. Then the children can cut out pictures of food items to place in their baskets.

Rainbow Ice

Things to talk about:

1. Is the sun hot or cold? Does the sun make us feel warm or cool? If it is hot enough, can heat melt things?
2. What can heat melt? Brainstorm! Possible answers are: ice cubes in a drink, snow, icebergs, ice over a lake, chocolate, candy, ice cream, and a snowman.
3. What melts and turns into water? (ice and snow)
4. When something melts, how does it change? It changes its shape and how it feels. For example, describe a candy bar. Now pretend it has been sitting in a hot car. It has melted. What words can you use to describe how it looks now? (Soft? Warm? Gooey?)

Materials:

Water, a large mixing bowl, food coloring, salt, a large shallow pan

Preparation:

Fill a bowl with water. Leave an inch from the top. Freeze it.

Things to do:

1. Place the bowl, inverted, under a running tap of warm water.
2. Then place the inverted bowl in the pan. Tap on the sides. The ice will slip down into the pan.
3. The children can take turns shaking on the salt. The salt will melt and make holes inside the ice.
4. Then have everyone drop on the food coloring. Watch the colors run and swirl.
5. Leave the ice in the tray. Observe how it looks as it melts down during the day.

More Ideas:

• Instead of making the ice bowl, you can buy a block of ice.
• Take pictures of the entire process, from the water in the bowl to the last meltdown. Post them on a wall and observe the sequence of events.

Hi Ho The Sun!

Things to talk about:

1. Ask the question: "What does the word connected mean?" As you say this, you can spread your fingers apart and interlock them together. Brainstorm! Connected can mean many pieces fitting together.

2. Everything on the earth is connected together. Talk about what this means. Help explain that the sun warms the earth and keeps everything from freezing. Trees give us shade. Cows give us milk. Bees make us honey. Think of other examples.

3. What do people do to help each other? We pick up litter. We grow vegetables. We donate blood. We build roads and parks.

4. During the hot summer months, what can we do to help other people or the earth? Offer someone a drink if they look thirsty. Help an older person carry a heavy package. Take a friend swimming. Water your grass. Make sure your house plants have enough water. Make sure your pets have water.

Materials: Poster board, sun pattern (page 28), yellow construction paper

Preparation: Make a poster board headband. Attach a yellow construction paper sun to the headband.

Things to do:

1. Stand in a circle. Hold hands. Choose a child to stand in the middle of the circle. This child is the summer sun. Have the child wear the sun headband.

2. Sing the following song to the tune of *The Farmer in the Dell*. Walk around in a circle as you sing. Each child can choose another child to stand inside the circle, as you would in *The Farmer in the Dell*.

3. The last child to stand in the circle is the honey. Then everyone returns to the circle except the child who is the honey. This child stands alone while the last verse is sung.

The sun loves the earth; the sun loves the earth,
Hi ho the derrio, the sun loves the earth.

The earth loves the tree, the earth loves the tree,
Hi ho the derrio, the earth loves the tree.

The tree loves the bird, the tree loves the bird,
Hi ho the derrio, the tree loves the bird.

The bird loves the flower, the bird loves the flower,
Hi ho the derrio, the bird loves the flower.

The flower loves the bee, the flower loves the bee,
Hi ho the derrio, the flower loves the bee.

The bee loves the honey, the bee loves the honey,
Hi ho the derrio, the bee loves the honey.

The honey stands alone, the honey stands alone,
Hi ho the derrio, the honey stands alone.

More Ideas:

• During the song, the children can think of different words. Try all animal words. Try different sea creatures. Try insects.

The Sunrise Game

Things to talk about:

1. During the summer, the days are long and sunny. What makes the day long? (The sun shines longer.)
2. Would you rather have a long day or a long night? If you had a long day, what would you do?
3. What happens when the sun rises? Brainstorm! Possible answers are: You wake up; It gets lighter outside; It gets warmer outside; Birds start to chirp; Animals wake up; You smell breakfast.
4. What happens when the sun sets? It gets darker. The air gets cooler. You can see the stars and the moon. You get ready for bed. You feel tired. People stay inside more. Stores close. Animals find a place to sleep.

Materials:

Yellow balloons, one for each child, recorded music

Preparation:

Blow up the balloons.

Things to do:

1. Sit in a circle. Give everyone a yellow balloon. Pretend that your balloon is the sun.
2. Have everyone place their balloon in their lap. Now hold onto your balloon and slowly move it above your head. The sun is rising. This is called a sunrise.
3. Now slowly bring the sun down, back to your lap. The sun is setting. This is called a sunset.
4. Now stand up. Play music. Have everyone dance with their sun balloons. Bat them in the air. Try to keep the sun rising.
5. If a balloon lands on the ground, the sun has set. Hurry and get it high in the sky.
6. When you feel tired, you can sit down and put your balloon in your lap. Your sun has set.

More Ideas:

• Use blue balloons for a rainstorm. When a blue balloon hits the ground, a raindrop has fallen. Use white balloons for snow falling.

The Summer Story

Things to talk about:

1. What does it mean to use your memory? Your memory helps you to remember things.
2. Where is your memory kept? In your brain. If you injure your brain, can you lose your memory?
3. Test your memory. Ask questions, such as: "What did you eat for breakfast?" "What do your pajamas look like?" "Can you describe your bedroom?"
4. Your memory helps you to remember stories. Who remembers the story, "The Three Little Pigs?" What animal chases the three little pigs?
5. Test your memory again. The teacher can say a word. For example: Caterpillar. Have everyone repeat the word. Your memory works fast.

Materials:

Pictures of the following items: the sun, trees, leaves, a green paper, buds, flowers, bees, butterflies, ladybugs, grass, a dog, the beach, people swimming, sailboats, surfers, people smiling

Preparation:

Collect the above pictures. Place them in a bag or box.

Things to do:

1. Tell *The Summer Story*. As you tell the story, show the objects in your bag that match certain words. For example: When you say the word leaves, show a picture of leaves.
2. When you have finished telling *The Summer Story*, tell it again. This time, hold up the items, but don't say their matching words. See if the children can remember the words in the story.

The Summer Story

The summer sun warms the earth. The sun helps trees to grow. Leaves are green. Buds grow into flowers. Bees hunt for flowers in the warm sun. Butterflies are in the air. Ladybugs decorate the grass.

Summer is a great time to walk your dog, go to the beach, go swimming, or ride your bike. Some people go camping, sail their sailboats or go surfing. Summer is a great time of year, and brings many happy smiles to many faces.

More Ideas:

- Have the children make up a summer story. Write down the story as each child makes up a part of it. Collect pictures to represent the story. Then tell their summer story.

Flowers Forever

Things to talk about:

1. Why are there so many flowers in summer? Flowers love heat and light.
2. If you pick a flower, what will happen to it? Why will it eventually die? What can you do to help it stay alive longer? Place it in a vase with water.
3. Why do people pick flowers? Possible answers are: to decorate their house; to give to someone; to place in their hair.
4. Is their a way to keep a flower forever? Brainstorm! (You can dry flowers and press them flat.)

Materials:

Flowers, tissue paper, heavy books.

Preparation:

Collect flowers, one for each child. The flowers should be fresh and dry, without dew or water on them

Things to do:

1. Sit in a circle. Place the flowers in the middle of the circle. Observe their different shapes and colors.
2. Press the flowers. Everyone can help. Place a large heavy book on the rug. Open a page in the middle of the book. (You might need two or three books.)
3. Place a sheet of tissue paper on the page. Now have each child choose a flower and place it on the tissue.
4. Take another sheet of tissue paper and place it over the flowers.
5. Close the book. Place a few heavy books on top of the book or books with flowers in them.
6. Leave the flowers in the books for four weeks.

More Ideas:

- Make a chart to count down the four weeks. Make it in a long strip or in a calendar design. The children can place a paper flower on each square, as the days pass.
- Make pictures, cards or bookmarks with the pressed flowers. Place them on construction paper, in pretty designs. Glue them on and cover them with plastic wrap. Trim the edges. Keep your creation or give it away as a gift.

Night Sky

Things to talk about:

1. Ask the question: "If you went stargazing, what would you be doing?" Looking at the stars. Who has stargazed? Where were you?

2. Stargazing only requires two things. What are they? Your eyes and a dark night sky.

3. What are stars? They are objects in the sky that give off light. They are hot. They are flaming balls of gas. If all the stars in the sky disappeared, would the night be darker or lighter?

4. What else in the sky gives us light? The moon. How many moons does the earth have? One. If the earth had 20 moons, would the sky be darker or lighter?

Materials:

Butcher paper, black paint, paintbrushes, tape, silver sticky stars

Preparation:

Paint a long sheet of butcher paper black. Tape it low on a wall. Place the stars all over the black paper. Place seven of the stars in the shape of the Big Dipper.

Things to do:

1. Darken the room. Sit quietly by your night sky. How do you feel when you look at the night sky? Calm?

2. Ask everyone to look for patterns in the stars. Can you see the shape of a dog? A horse? A flower? Explain that patterns of stars are called constellations.

3. Explain that this is a summer night sky. Each season, there are different stars in the sky. In the summer sky, there is a group of stars that look like a big dipper. It is called The Big Dipper. Can anyone see it? It looks like a big soup spoon.

4. Draw lines with a felt pen, connecting the stars in The Big Dipper.

5. Children can take turns pointing to the seven stars and counting them.

More Ideas:

• Children can take turns connecting stars with a felt pen. Then they can think of a name for their constellation.

The Insect Chant

Things to talk about:

1. Everyone gets excited about summer. Why do you think people look forward to summer? Brainstorm. Possible reasons might be: Many people like warm weather; People take vacations during the summer; The days are longer; You can do more things.
2. Who else likes summer? (besides people.) Clap your hands. (Clap after each new thought) Bees like summer. Butterflies like summer. Flowers like summer. Apple trees like summer. Vegetable gardens like summer.
3. Why do you think people write songs about summer? It is a way to celebrate summer.

Materials: None

Preparation: None

Things to do:

Learn *The Insect Chant* to celebrate insects. Do the suggested movements.

For the words "butterfly": Move fingers up and down and around in the air.
For the words "ladybug": Move thumb and first finger up and down and all around.
For the words "dragonfly": Cross both first fingers and move around.
For the words "bumblebee": Move fists around in the air.

For the words, "flying in the air": Keep flying your insect.
For the words "Oh, no!": Place both hands on your cheeks.
For the words, "It landed in my hair!": Touch your hair.
Give a nice long sigh for the word "sigh."

The Insect Chant

Butterfly, butterfly,
Flying in the air.
Oh no! Oh no!
It landed in my hair!
(sigh)

Ladybug, ladybug,
Flying in the air.
Oh no! Oh no!
It landed in my hair!
(sigh)

Dragonfly, dragonfly,
Flying in the air.
Oh no! Oh no!
It landed in my hair!
(sigh)

Bumblebee, bumblebee,
Flying in the air.
Oh no! Oh no!
It landed in my hair!
(scream!)

More Ideas:

• Extend the verses. The children can think of more insects or birds to land in your hair.

Fire Brainstorms

Help. There is a fire.

Things to talk about:

1. If you see matches, what should you do? Leave them alone. Why is fire dangerous? It can burn you. It can destroy many things: houses, buildings, cars, and even forests.
2. Why is fire especially dangerous during hot weather? If grass and trees are dry, from no rain, a fire can spread fast.
3. Is it safe to build a campfire? How should you put out a campfire? Pour water on the hot coals and rocks. Make sure it is completely out.
4. Is it safe to drop a burning match or piece of paper in a trash can? Why not?
5. If you see a fire, what should you do? Brainstorm! Possible answers are: Alert an adult; Call the fire department; Stay away from it.

Materials:

A stopwatch, a toy phone, blocks, red plastic-wrap

Preparation: None

Things to do:

Listed below are some "hot," ideas to encourage fire safety.

- Practice Stop, Drop and Roll, in case your clothes catch on fire. Sit in a circle. Everyone, in turn, can stand in the middle of the circle. The remaining children can say: "Stop!" The child freezes. Then "drop!" The child drops to the rug. Then "roll!" The child rolls back and forth, on the rug, covering his or her face.
- Have a fire drill, but with a stopwatch. Have the children walk around the classroom. When you yell fire, everyone can quickly walk to the assigned door and form a line. Announce your 'Drill time.' Do it again. See if you can beat your time.
- Sit in a circle. Choose a child to look out a window. This child can yell, "fire!" Choose a child to dial the emergency number for your area. Take turns yelling fire and dialing for help.
- Make a pretend campfire. Pile blocks on the rug to form a wood. Place crinkled up red or pink plastic wrap around the blocks, for the fire. Now sit around your campfire. Warm your hands. Talk about the good things that fire can do (light birthday candles, cook food, and warm you by a fireplace.) When you are finished, everyone can help take apart the fire.

More Ideas:

- Make S'Mores in a toaster oven. Turn off the lights. Sit around a pretend campfire and tell stories.

Summer Do's And Don'ts!

Things to talk about:

1. Ask the question: "What are some things that you can Do in a classroom?" Possible answers are: Play with your friends; eat your lunch; paint; draw; sing; look at books; talk to your teacher.

2. Ask the question: "What are some things that you Don't Do in a classroom?" Answers might be: Run; yell; hurt your friends; throw toys; tear books; make a mess and not clean up; drop food on the floor; play a mean trick on someone.

3. Why are there Do's and Don'ts in a classroom? Following rules and making good decisions help to keep us safe and healthy.

4. Are there Do's and Don't outside of the classroom? Brainstorm! Possible answers might be: In your car; In your home; At a movie theatre; At the beach; In a store.

Materials:

White butcher paper, scissors, double-sided tape, red and green paper, a felt pen

Preparation:

Cut a large sheet of butcher paper. Tape it low on a wall. Draw two large circles, side by side. Label one circle "Do's" and one circle "Don'ts." Cut out Do and Don't circles (page 37) from red and green paper. Cut out at least one red and green circle for each child. (Place double-sided tape all over each circle so you can easily stick things on.)

Things to do:

1. Explain that there are many things to do in summer. Some of these things are Do's and some are Don'ts.

2. Give each child a red and green circle. Explain that the green circle represents a Do. The red circle represents a Don't.

3. Read from a list of questions concerning Summer Do's and Don'ts. Everyone can take a turn answering a question. If the answer is a Do, the child can stick a green circle inside the circle labeled Do. If the answer is a Don't, the child can stick a red circle inside the circle labeled Don't. Talk briefly about why it is a Do or a Don't.

4. Suggested questions are:

- If you get too hot, the best thing to do is drink water. (Do)
- If you can't swim, you can go in the shallow end of a pool without an adult. (Don't!)
- If the sun hurts your eyes, you can wear sunglasses. (Do)
- The summer sun is so bright and pretty. It is okay to look at it. (Don't)
- If you get stung by a bee, tell a grown-up. (Do)
- If you see a dog that you do not know, it is okay to pet it. (Don't)
- If you are playing at a park, and someone asks you if you want to see the puppies in their car, run away from them. (Do)
- If you are playing with your ball, and it rolls into the street, you can run and get it. (Don't)
- If you are outside and it is very hot, you should put suntan lotion on. (Do)
- It is okay to drink ocean water. (Don't)
- If you see an anthill, watch them. Try not to disturb their work. (Do)
- If you see an interesting looking bug or spider, pick it up. (Don't)
- If you catch a bug and want to observe it for awhile, poke holes in the lid of the jar. (Do)
- If you go on a picnic, leave your food out on your plate, if you want to go play. (Don't)

Red **Green**

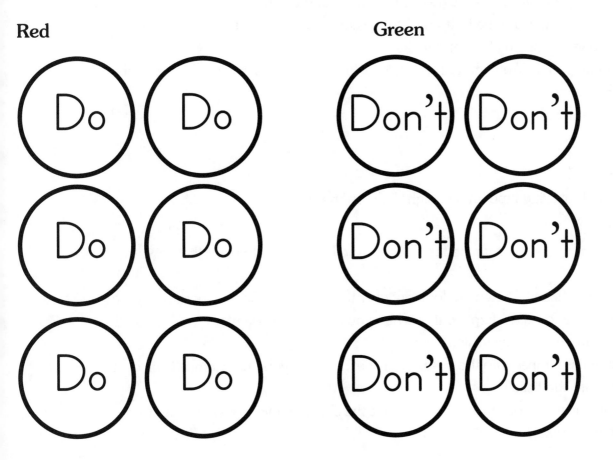

More Ideas:
- Take a Summer Do and Don't walk. Observe things you see that are okay to Do. Look for things that could be a Don't. Talk about them when you return to class.

What's A Beach?

Things to talk about:

1. Ask the question: "Who has been to a beach?" Then ask, "What is a beach?" A beach is the sandy area alongside an ocean.

2. How does a beach get there? Does a giant truck pour sand on the ground? Brainstorm! Sand can be washed up from the bottom of the ocean. Sand can be formed when the ocean pounds away at nearby land and rocks.

3. Why do you think people like to go to the beach? Would you like to live in a house on the beach? Why? Why not?

Materials:

Masking tape

Preparation:

Tape a long strip of masking tape, in a straight line, on the rug.

Things to do:

1. Have everyone sit on one side of the tape. This is the beach side. Explain that the other side is the ocean.

2. Now have everyone stand. Pretend to look out over the "ocean." Ask the question: "Who wants to jump in the ocean?" Explain that when you say, ocean, everyone can jump off the beach and land on the ocean side.

3. When everyone has jumped into the ocean, yell "beach!" Everyone now jumps back over the tape, and onto the beach.

4. Continue to say the words ocean and beach, while the children follow directions and jump into the matching area.

More Ideas:

• Choose a child to be the lifeguard. When the children are in the ocean, the lifeguard can yell, "shark!" The children then jump out of the water and safely rest on the beach.

• Lay blue butcher paper over the ocean side. Two children, at a time, can swim in the ocean. On the teacher's signal, the children on the beach can yell, "shark!"

Something Invisible!

Things to talk about:

1. Show everyone your hand. Ask if everyone can see your hand. Now place your hand behind your back. Ask the question: "Is my hand invisible?" No. It is only hiding.
2. What does the word invisible mean? Something is there but you can't see it. Look at the air all around you. You can't see it, but you can feel it when you fan yourself. Look at the germs on the palm of your hand. They are so tiny, they seem invisible.
3. Explain that there is something invisible at the ocean. Brainstorm. Is it an invisible fish? An invisible pirate ship? There is an invisible line at the ocean. It separates the ocean from the beach.
4. Ask everyone to use their imaginations. Look at the rug. Can you imagine a long line on the rug? Move your finger along the rug to help the children visualize the line.

Materials:

Masking tape

Preparation:

Stick a long line of masking tape on the rug.

Things to do:

1. Have the children sit on one side of the tape. Explain that there is an invisible line at the ocean. The line is right where the water ends and the beach begins. It is called the shoreline.
2. Demonstrate. The teacher can walk along the tape. Pretend that one side is the water and the other side is the sand. Dip your foot in the water. It's cold. Stay walking along the shoreline. If you move off the line, you will get your feet wet.
3. Everyone, in turn, can walk along the shoreline. Try to balance on the line. If you walk off the line, on the water side, you will get wet.

More Ideas:

• Think of different ways to walk along the shoreline. Suggestions are: walk backwards; walk on tiptoes; or jog along the shore.

Things to talk about:

1. Why does ocean water taste salty? It has salt in it. Where does the salt come from? Brainstorm! Then tell The Salt Story. It comes from rocks on the land. Rain washes the salt off the rocks and into rivers. The rivers carry it to the oceans. See who can repeat The Salt Story.

2. Who has tasted salt? How did you taste it? From a saltshaker? On food? Did you like the taste?

3. What kind of food have you tasted with salt on it? Brainstorm! Possible answers might be: potato chips, pretzels, popcorn, corn and watermelon.

4. How does salt make food taste? Salty. What would not taste good with salt on it? Milk? Popsicles? Cereal?

Materials:

A clear container, an egg, water, salt

Preparation: None

Things to do:

1. Explain that salt, in water, can make objects float. Demonstrate.
   - Pour water in a transparent glass or container, halfway up.
   - Carefully place a raw egg in the glass.
   - Now slowly pour salt in. Watch the egg. It will rise to the surface.

2. Taste cut-up watermelon, or some other type of food. Now taste it with salt sprinkled on it. Which way do you like it better?

3. Place a tiny bit of sugar on the tip of one finger. Place a tiny bit of salt on the tip of another finger. Lick. How do they each taste? Which is your favorite?

More Ideas:

- Make salt water pictures. Spread glue on a sheet of paper. Sprinkle salt over the glue. When the glue has dried, paint over the salt with blue and green paint.

The Sink Or Float Scientist

Things to talk about:

1. Ask the question: "If you jumped into a pool and you didn't swim, would you sink or float?" "Why would you sink?" Your body is heavier than the water.
2. Place an ice cube in a bowl of water. Does the ice cube sink or float? It floats because it is lighter than water.
3. Think of things that float in water. Possible ideas are: boats, canoes, rafts, balloons, ice cubes, plastic toys, cardboard boxes, paper plates, a twig, and leaves.
4. Think of things that sink in water. These might be: rocks, a brick, a spoon, keys, a coin, a marble, a wooden block, a bar of soap, canned food, and a seashell.

Materials:

A large shallow pan, water, a paper bag, objects that sink or float

Preparation:

Fill a pan with water. Collect items that sink or float. Place the items in a paper bag.

Things to talk about:

1. Sit in a circle. Place the pan of water in the middle of the circle.
2. Choose a child to be The Sink or Float Scientist. This child can pick an item from the paper bag.
3. The child can look at the item and guess if it will sink or float.
4. Now the child can place the item in the pan. Watch what happens.
5. Give everyone a chance to be The Sink or Float Scientist.

More Ideas:

- Post two charts on the wall. Label them: "Things that Float," and "Things that Sink." Print the items on the charts as you observe which ones sink or float.
- Have each child bring an item from home. Use these items to sink or float in the pan of water.

Ten At Sea

Things to talk about:

1. Talk about rhythm! Clap your hands slowly, with a two second pause between claps. Now clap faster. Try a more complicated rhythm. Clap once, followed by two short claps.
2. Try clapping as you name sea animals. Clap as you say whale. Continue to clap as you say different sea animals.
3. Have the children pick three sea animals. Then clap as you say each one. Memorize the three animal words and repeat the chant, over and over.
4. Now count to ten. Then count backwards from ten to one. Clap as you count.

Materials: None

Preparation: None

Things to do:

1. Say the following chant to the tune of *Ten in The Bed and the Little One Said Roll Over*. Clap as you say it.
2. When you say the words "meet at the beach," place your hands around your mouth and yell them.
3. Now go on a swim with your ten ocean friends. As each friend leaves you, one at a time, to meet at the beach, you find yourself swimming with less and less friends. What happens when all of you are at the beach? Find out.

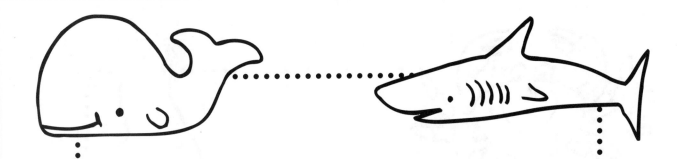

Ten at sea,
And along with me,
Who's coming! Who's coming!
The whale said,
Meet at the beach.

Nine at sea,
And along with me,
Who's coming! Who's coming!
The shark said,
Meet at the beach.

Eight at sea,
And along with me,
Who's coming! Who's coming!
The dolphin said,
Meet at the beach.

Seven at sea,
And along with me,
Who's coming! Who's coming!
The octopus said,
Meet at the beach.

Six at sea,
And along with me,
Who's coming! Who's coming!
The eel said,
Meet at the beach.

Five at sea,
And along with me,
Who's coming! Who's coming!
The lobster said,
Meet at the beach.

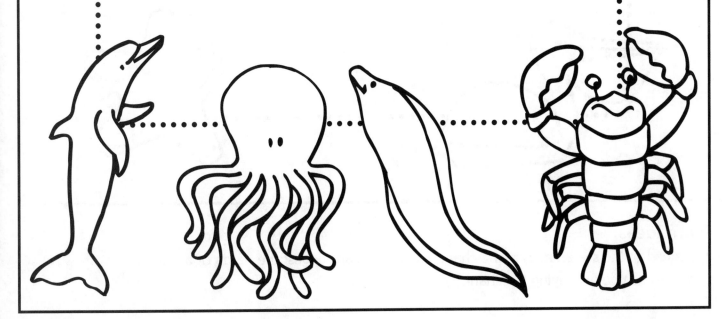

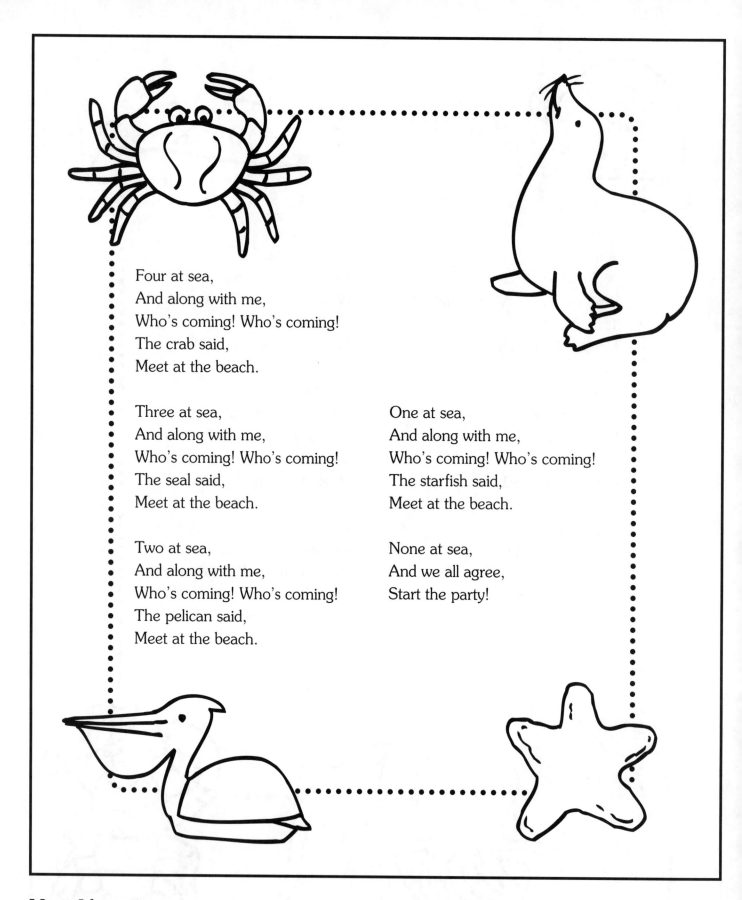

Four at sea,
And along with me,
Who's coming! Who's coming!
The crab said,
Meet at the beach.

Three at sea,
And along with me,
Who's coming! Who's coming!
The seal said,
Meet at the beach.

Two at sea,
And along with me,
Who's coming! Who's coming!
The pelican said,
Meet at the beach.

One at sea,
And along with me,
Who's coming! Who's coming!
The starfish said,
Meet at the beach.

None at sea,
And we all agree,
Start the party!

More Ideas:

• Instead of the sea animals in the chant, each child can suggest the name of a sea animal as you are saying the chant.

Submarine Ride

Things to talk about:

1. Ask the questions: "Can you live under the ocean?" "Why not?"
2. Ask a mystery riddle. There is something you can ride in. Brainstorm! It can take you under the sea. You can live inside of it for many days? What is it? A submarine.
3. Why can you live underwater in a submarine? (It is airtight. Water does not leak in. You breathe air inside the submarine. There is a kitchen, beds and bathroom.)
4. Are there windows in a submarine? Do you open them?
5. There is a door in a submarine. When would you open the door in a submarine? (When you are above water.)

Materials:

Butcher paper, scissors, tape, markers

Preparation:

Cut a long sheet of butcher. Tape it low on a wall. Draw a submarine on it. Draw at least four large portholes.

Things to do:

1. Play a game called "I Rode in a Submarine." The teacher begins the game by saying: I rode in a submarine and I saw a (_____.) The teacher fills in the blank. For example, the teacher might say a whale.
2. Then a child, to the left of the teacher, repeats the teacher's sentence and adds something that he or she saw. The sentence might now be: I rode in a submarine and I saw a whale and a mermaid.
3. Each child can repeat the original sentence, adding all the items already said, plus their new item.
4. The last child will say all the items mentioned, plus one last item.

More Ideas:

• Have the children, a few at a time, pretend to look through the portholes. Then place a variety of markers on the rug. They can draw, in the portholes, what they see in the ocean.

Gulp! Gulp! Gulp!

Things to talk about:

1. What are you? A bird? A fish? A human? Do you breathe air? Have everyone take a deep breathe. We breathe oxygen from the air.
2. Do fish need oxygen? Yes. They take it from the water.
3. How do fish breathe in oxygen? Do they have noses? (As fish swim, they gulp in water and push it out through slits on their heads. These slits are called gills. Oxygen from the water enters the fish.)
4. Do all sea creatures breathe underwater? No. Sea lions, seals, dolphins and whales breathe air.
5. If they breathe air, what do they have to do, if they live in the water? They have to surface and take a breathe of air.

Materials:

Yarn, scissors

Preparation:

Cut a long string of yarn. Secure it above and across your circle time area to represent the ocean.

Things to do:

1. Observe the yarn. Pretend the yarn is the surface of the ocean. You are fish under the ocean.
2. Explain that fish swim by moving their muscles, along their body, in a rippling motion. Practice this motion. Have everyone kneel, so your heels are touching your seat. Now slowly wiggle upward, until your thighs are straight. Wiggle up and down, in a kneeling position.
3. A fish turns left and right by moving his fins. Wiggle up. Have everyone bend arms at the elbows with hands out to the side. They are now fins. Together, move to the left and right.
4. You need air. Have everyone gulp.
5. Now you are a dolphin. Swim upward until you are standing above the yarn line. Take a deep breathe. Then slowly lower yourself under the ocean. Don't gulp.

More Ideas:

• Tape a large sheet of butcher paper low on a wall. Draw a large fish on the paper. Add scales and gills. When you have finished the activity, everyone can color in the fish.

Fishy Questions

Things to talk about:

1. Ask the following questions: "What part of you do you smell with?" "What part of you do you see with?" "What do you feel with?" "What do you hear with?"

2. Now ask: "What part of you do you think with?" Your brain. Where is it? Place the palms of your hands on your head. Your brain is at the top part of your body, inside your head.

3. See if your brain is working. Ask everyone to answer the following question. Everyone can yell out the answer at the same time: "When you are hungry, what do you want to do?" (Eat!)

4. Your brains are working. Your brain is what you think with. Now your brain is warmed up and ready to answer some very fishy questions.

Material

A container, paper, a pen.

Preparation:

Cut strips of paper, a few inches long. Cut one for each child.

Print an ocean question on each strip. Place these strips in the container.

Things to do:

Everyone, in turn, can choose a question from the container and try to answer it. Clap after each answer. Suggested questions are:

- What has eight arms and lives in the ocean?
- What is the largest sea animal in the ocean and can grow to be 100 feet long? A hint. It begins with the word, blue. (a blue whale)
- What sea animal swims up and down, like a merry-go-round horse? (a sea horse)
- What warms the ocean waters? (the sun)
- What is in the ocean that makes it taste salty?
- Why do we call a certain shark, hammerhead shark? (Its head looks like a hammer.)
- Is it light or dark at the bottom of the sea? Why? (Sunlight doesn't reach that far down.)
- Why do dolphins have sharp teeth? (To hold onto slippery fish.)
- Are there mountains under the ocean? (Yes. They are called volcanoes)

More Ideas:

- Decorate your container with ocean pictures or stickers.
- Place a fish sticker on each child as they answer a question.

Musical Fish

Things to talk about:

1. Ask the question: "Why do we play games?" Brainstorm! Possible answers are: We learn things from games. We can learn how to count, keep a rhythm, play fair and take turns.
2. What is the most important reason why we play games? To have fun.
3. Why is it important to follow the rules of a game? Rules tell us how to play a game. If one person does not follow the rules, it is not fair to all the other game players.
4. Is it fun to win a game? Yes. Is it the most important part of a game? No. What is the most important part of a game? To have fun.

Materials:

Chairs, one for each child, masking tape

Preparation:

Tape a large circle on the rug, with the masking tape. Make the circle large enough for all the children to sit in.

Things to do:

Below are suggestions for group games with a fishy theme.

1. Play Musical Fish. This game is similar to Musical Chairs. Arrange chairs in two rows, back to back. Make a large circle on the rug, with yarn or masking tape. This is the whale's belly. Have everyone sit in a chair. Play music. The children are fish, who swim around the chairs. Take a chair away while everyone is swimming. Then stop the music. Everyone can swim to a chair. The child who is left without a chair to sit in, is swallowed by the whale and sits in the whale's belly. The last child is the fish who got away.
2. Play Freeze fish. This is played like Freeze Dance. Make a large circle on the rug with yarn or tape. Everyone can stand inside the circle. Now play music. When you stop the music, freeze. If you see a child who moves, tag the child on the shoulder. This child then sits down in the shark's mouth. Play until you have one child standing.
3. Play Ring Around The Fishes. Hold hands in a circle. As you walk around, sing the following chant to the tune of *Ring Around The Roses*:

> Ring around the fishes,
> Pocket full of wishes.
> Bubbles, bubbles,
> We all float down.

More Ideas:

As an option, play this game over and over. Change the word float to different types of movement, such as, sink, swim and dive.

Circle Time—Summer • ©2004 Monday Morning Books, Inc.

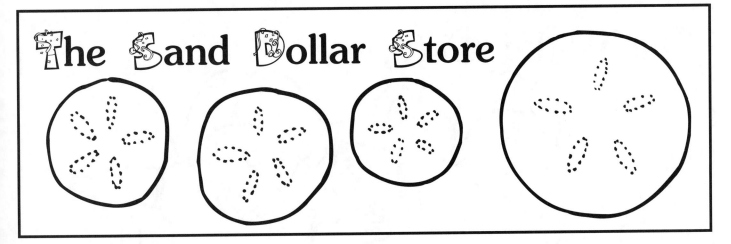

The Sand Dollar Store

Things to talk about:

1. Show a sand dollar, or a picture of one. Ask the question: "What is a sand dollar?" It is a sea creature. Why do you think it is called a sand dollar? (It is round, like a silver dollar. It is often found in sand.)
2. Does a sand dollar have arms or legs? How do you think it moves around? Brainstorm! (It has a layer of fine hair on its body. When these spines move around, the sand dollar moves.)
3. Would it be hard to move without arms and legs? Lay flat on the rug. Try to move without the use of your limbs.
4. Sand dollars have different designs in the middle of their shell. If you were a sand dollar, what design would you like on you?

Materials:

White posterboard, scissors, felt pens, items from the classroom

Preparation:

Draw sand dollars on the posterboard. Cut them out. Make at least one for each child.

Things to do:

1. Give each child one or more sand dollars. Print each child's name on the underside of their dollars. Place felt pens on a table. Everyone can draw designs on their sand dollars.
2. Place the sand dollars in a box. Set up a Sand Dollar Store. Place items from the class room on the rug. Sit around the items.
3. Give a child the box of sand dollars. Ask the children what he or she would like to buy? The child can choose an item on the rug. The teacher can then say: It will cost five sand dollars. The child counts out five dollars and gives them to the teacher. She can then hold the item she has bought.
4. Continue until everyone has bought an item from the Sand Dollar Store. If the box runs low on sand dollars, place some of them back in the box.

More Ideas:

• Tape a sheet of yellow butcher paper low on a wall. Tape the sand dollars on the paper. Make a sign on the paper that reads: Sand Dollar Beach. How many do you see?

Ouch The Octopus

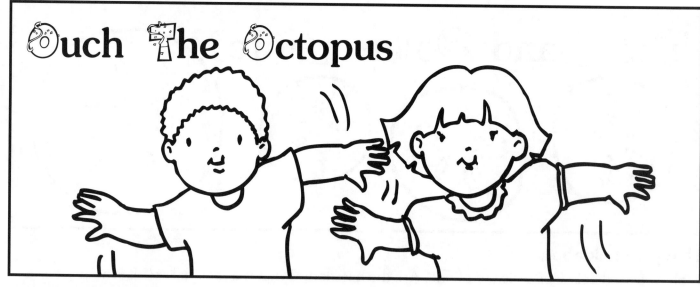

Things to talk about:

1. What is an octopus? It is a sea creature. It breathes underwater. It has eight arms.

2. What does an octopus do with his eight arms. Brainstorm! (He holds onto things with a tight grasp.) Have everyone take one hand and hold onto their other wrist. Hold on tight. Turn to a child next to you. See if this child can separate your hands. Take turns. Imagine how strong an octopus is with eight arms.

3. An octopus can camouflage itself. What does that mean? He can change colors and match an object he is sitting on. Children can look at their own clothes. What color would you be sitting on, if you were an octopus?

Materials: None

Preparation: None

Things to do:

1. Learn the chant Ouch the Octopus. Add body movements.

> Ouch the Octopus went to play (*clap hands*)
> Out of his cave, (*wiggle fingers*)
> All day, (*wiggle fingers*)
> And every day, his mother would shout, (*clap hands*)
> Watch out! (*wag a finger in the air*)

2. Now pretend to be Ouch the Octopus. Swim around, moving your arms up and down.

3. At an unsuspecting moment, the teacher yells, "Ouch!" Fling both hands in the air.

4. Choose a child to answer the question: How many arms did Ouch hurt?

5. If the number is five, slap each hand on the opposite arm, alternating back and forth, while you count to five. (Slap your underarm. It is an easier movement.)

6. Repeat the chant. Give everyone a turn to choose a number.

More Ideas:

• Choose a child to be the mother. This child can yell, "Watch out!"

     Circle Time—Summer • ©2004 Monday Morning Books, Inc.

Flounder Camouflage

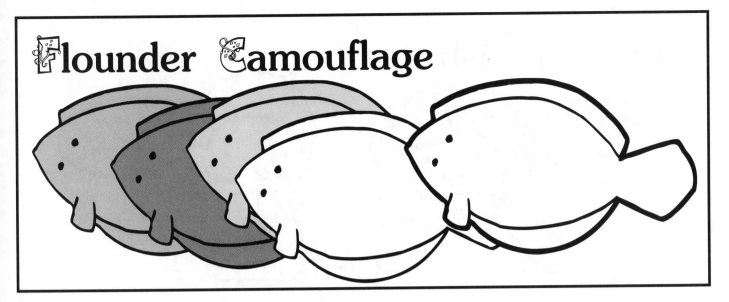

Things to talk about:

1. Pretend to walk in white snow. Move your hands on the rug, up and down. Now pretend to bump into a white rabbit. Ask the questions: "What happened?" "Why couldn't we see the white rabbit?" (It was camouflaged.)

2. What does camouflage mean? Something is hard to see. Its shape or color matches something that it is near. Ask the question: "If you were a red fox, and you didn't want hunters to see you, would you hide inside a bush with green leaves or red leaves?"

3. Ask similar questions. "If you were a green caterpillar, would you hide in green grass or yellow grass?" "If you were a purple butterfly, would you hide on an orange flower or a purple flower?" "If you were a white cloud, and you didn't want anyone to see you, would you hide in a blue sky or a white sky?"

Materials:

Colored construction paper, scissors, a felt pen

Preparation:

Cut out the shape of a flounder. Trace this shape on different colored paper. Cut out each flounder. Make one for each child.

Things to do:

1. Place different colored construction paper on the rug. Place a matching pile of flounders on the rug.

2. Explain to the children that flounders blend into the sand. If they are frightened, they will bury down and lay still. You can't see them.

3. Point to the flounders. These flounders are scared. Scuba divers are near and want to catch them. Choose a child to pick up a flounder and place it on a matching sheet of paper. For example: The red flounder is now hiding in red sand.

4. Continue to camouflage the remaining flounders.

More Ideas:

• Place only four to six matching papers and flounders on the rug. Mix them up. Take turns placing the flounders on their matching sand beds, as quickly as you can.

Tin Foil Fish

Things to talk about:

1. Ask the question: "How did you get your name?" Then ask: "How did all the different fish in the ocean get their names?"

2. Someone discovered each type of fish. Pretend you are swimming in the ocean. You look down and see a fish no one has ever seen before. Wow! You tell people who study the ocean. They might be scientists or oceanographers. They think of a name for the new fish. They might ask you to think of a name.

3. Show a book of sea creatures. Listen to the interesting names. Some names reflect what the fish looks like. A sea horse looks like a horse.

4. If you discovered a large red fish with stripes, what would be a good name for it? A candy cane fish? A red zebra fish? Brainstorm!

Materials:

Tin foil

Preparation:

Tear sheets out from the tin foil roll. Make one for each child.

Things to do:

1. Sit in a circle. Give each child a sheet of tin foil.
2. Explain that everyone can make a new species of fish. You are the first person to discover it.
3. Demonstrate how to easily twist and turn tin foil to create designs.
4. Make the newly discovered fish.
5. Everyone, in turn, can show their fish and name it.

More Ideas:

• Sit on a large sheet of blue butcher paper. Pretend you are sitting in the ocean. Make your fish and set them free. Observe all the beautiful new fish swimming in the ocean.
• Make tin foil sea monsters.

Land Ahoy!

Things to talk about:

1. How would it feel to spend a whole year on a boat? Would it be fun? Would you get bored? Would it ever feel scary?
2. Slowly sway back and forth. Why do you feel a swaying motion on a boat?
3. How would you get your food to eat? How would you get water to drink?
4. Why should you have life vests or rafts on board? Why should you have a radio on board?
5. What would you miss the most, if you lived on a boat? Brainstorm!

Materials:

An empty plastic bottle

Preparation: None

Things to do:

1. Play the game called "Land Ahoy!" Sit in a circle. Place the bottle in the middle of the circle.
2. Sing the following song to the tune of The Itsy Bitsy Spider. Below are suggested body movements:

My sailboat is sailing for days and days and days. (sway back and forth)

I'm getting tired of looking at the waves. (move hands up and down in a wavy motion)

I can feel some rain and a storm is coming near, (wiggle fingers, moving hands down)

So hold on tight, (grab sides of a steering wheel)

And don't let go of the wheel. (turn it back and forth)

3. The teacher now spins the bottle. When it stops and points to a child, the teacher says: How many miles to land? If the child answers 10, count to 10 as you rotate your wrists around and around each other. This is your boat engine on full speed.
4. When you finish counting, move hands upward in a climbing motion, place a hand over your eyes and yell, Land Ahoy!
5. Repeat the chant. Give everyone a turn to answer how many miles to land.

More Ideas:

- Substitute sailboat for pirate ship. Wear eye patches. At the end of the chant, the teacher yells: "The ships sinking! Walk the plank!" A child can walk along a board and jump off. She can resume sitting in the circle. Give everyone a turn to walk the plank.

Things to talk about:

1. What is the largest sea creature in the ocean? The whale. Is the whale a fish or a mammal? It is a mammal. It breathes air, just like us. Take a deep breath.
2. Pretend to be a pod of whales. Close your eyes. Imagine how it would feel to be so BIG. Now open your eyes. How did it feel? What would be hard to do, in the ocean, if you were as big as a whale?
3. What kind of a noise do you think a whale makes? Make each of the following noises: Whales hum. Whales whine. Whales squeak.
4. The blue whale is the largest whale in the ocean. What would be a good name for a blue whale? Brainstorm!

Materials:

Butcher paper, tape, scissors, a felt pen

Preparation:

Draw a large whale on the paper. By the whale, print the words, "A Whale's Tale." Below this title, print sentences, leaving blanks at the end. These blanks will be filled in by the children.

Things to do:

After each child has finished a sentence, print their name to the left of the number. Then read the tale. Possible sentences are listed below:

1. My name is _____.
2. I love being a whale because _____.
3. All day long I _____.
4. My favorite thing to do is _____.
5. My best friend is a _____.
6. We like to _____.
7. Sometimes I get scared when _____.
8. At night, I like to _____.
9. Sometimes, I wish _____.

More Ideas:

• Choose different sea animals to make-up stories about.

Sea Cave Explorers

Things to talk about:

1. Has anyone ever seen a sea cave? (In a book, on TV, on the side of a hill?)
2. How is a sea cave made? Brainstorm! A cave can be above water. It is carved by the waves. Waves throw sand and rocks against the cliff. Eventually, a deep hole is formed. It becomes a cave.
3. Is it light or dark inside a cave? Would a sea cave be dry or damp?
4. If you saw a cave by the sea, would you go inside? What do you think you would see inside a sea cave?
5. What would you do with a sea cave? Make a store inside of it? Paint it? Take pictures of it? Read a book by it? How about explore it.

Materials:

Yellow and gray construction paper, a sheet, tape, a flashlight

Preparation:

Drape a sheet over a table. This is a sea cliff. Crunch up sheets of yellow and gray paper. These are sand and rock balls. Have the children help. Place them on the rug by the table.

Things to do:

1. Sit by the long side of the table. This side is your sea cliff. Pretend you are sea waves. Pick up the balls of sand and rock and throw them at the cliff. Throw them over and over.
2. After a few minutes, grab the bottom edge of the sheet between two fingers. Pull this part up and tape it to the top of the table. You have made an opening in the cliff. You have carved out a cave.
3. Explore the cave? Crawl inside. Shine a flashlight. Look all around. What do you see? Do you feel cold? Hot?
4. If you have a large group, make two sea caves from two tables. You can also place the tables in a row. Crawl through your sea cave. Rest in it.

More Ideas:

• Have a sea cave day. Tape butcher paper all over the classroom to form many caves. The children can play in the sea caves all day.

Things to talk about:

1. Are there plants under the ocean? Yes. Kelp or seaweed grows under the ocean.
2. Place a potted plant on the rug. Stare at it. Can you see it grow? It grows too slow to see. Kelp is the fastest growing plant in the world. You could watch kelp grow.
3. Can you see kelp above the water? It is so long, that you can see it twirling around and around at the surface of the ocean. It also washes up on the beach.
4. How would kelp be a danger to scuba divers? Divers can get trapped in the kelp, below or above the water.
5. People use seaweed for many things. (They put seaweed in vitamins, shampoo, face cream, paint, soup and ice cream.) Act these things out and see if anyone can guess what you are doing.

Materials:

Green crepe paper.

Preparation:

Cut strips of crepe paper, at least a foot long. Cut one for each child. Pretend the strips are seaweed.

Things to do:

1. Sing the following song to the tune of *There's a Spider on My Head*. As you sing it, drape your seaweed over the matching body part.
2. After the first verse, take the seaweed off your head and drop it on the floor.

There is seaweed on my head, on my head.
There is seaweed on my head, on my head.
There is seaweed on my head, and it's something that I dread,
There is seaweed on my head, on my head!

Circle Time—Summer • ©2004 Monday Morning Books, Inc.

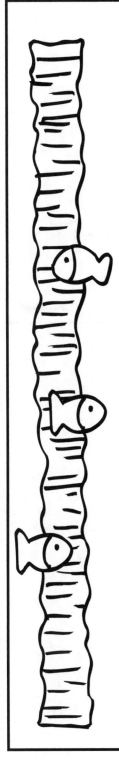

There is seaweed on the floor, on the floor.
There is seaweed on the floor, on the floor.
There is seaweed on the floor, someone sweep it out the door,
There is seaweed on the floor, on the floor!

There is seaweed on my thigh, on my thigh.
There is seaweed on my thigh, on my thigh.
There is seaweed on my thigh, and I think that I will die,
There is seaweed on my thigh, on my thigh!

There is seaweed on my tummy, on my tummy.
There is seaweed on my tummy, on my tummy.
There is seaweed on my tummy, and I do not think it's funny,
There is seaweed on my tummy, on my tummy!

There is seaweed on my arm, on my arm.
There is seaweed on my arm, on my arm.
There is seaweed on my arm, and I'm feeling quite alarmed,
There is seaweed on my arm, on my arm!

There is seaweed on my neck, on my neck.
There is seaweed on my neck, on my neck.
There is seaweed on my neck, and I think I am a wreck,
There is seaweed on my neck, on my neck!

There is seaweed on my head, on my head.
There is seaweed on my head, on my head.
There is seaweed on my head, and I think that I am dead,
There is seaweed on my head, on my head!

More Ideas:

- This will take a large roll of green crepe paper. Wrap a child up in seaweed. On the count of three, the child can burst out. Give everyone a turn to get caught in the seaweed.
- Lay the seaweed in a circular pattern on the rug. Take turns trying to walk through the seaweed and not step on it.

School Harbor

Things to talk about:

1. What's a harbor? Brainstorm! A harbor is a place where boats dock.
2. Water, in a harbor, is usually calm. Why? It is built near the land. You sail out of a harbor to sail across the ocean or go for a long ride.
3. Some people live at a harbor. They live on their boats. Would you like to live on a boat? Why? Why not?
4. There is often a pier at a harbor. A pier is a walkway that sticks out over the water. It is long and narrow like a sidewalk. If you walked along a pier, what do you think you might see? Possible answers are: sailboats, motorboats, fishing boats, nets, dogs, a pelican, fish, fisherman, seafood restaurants, and a harbor patrol boat.

Materials:

Blue butcher paper or construction paper, white paper or posterboard, a felt pen, tape, wooden blocks, toy boats and people figures - (optional)

Preparation:

Tape a large sheet of blue paper on the rug. Tape the posterboard on a wall, near the blue paper. Label it: Harbor Activities (7 to 5) or the hours of your school.

Things to do:

1. Sit around the blue paper. This is ocean water. Build a harbor around it.
2. Place the wooden blocks off to one side. Choose a child to begin building.
3. This builder can place a block anywhere along the water. You can build piers, sidewalks, stores, or use some blocks for boats.

4. Pretend to visit your harbor. Brainstorm things you might do there. Print them on your Harbor Activity Sign. Ideas might be:

- Take sailing lessons
- Go whale watching
- Take a boat tour of the harbor
- Rent paddle boats or kyacks
- Go fishing off the pier
- Eat at a fish restaurant
- Watch fishing boats pull in

More Ideas:
- Post a sign with the name of your harbor on it. If the name of your school is: Rainbow Bridge, the sign can read: Welcome to Rainbow Bridge Harbor.
- Children can bring things from home to add to the harbor, such as, toy boats, ships, and figures of people or animals.

Build A Beach House

Things to do:

1. Talk about different places that you can live. Brainstorm! Answers might be: in a city, out in the country, on a farm, in a mobile home, in a cabin in the mountains, in a house on the beach, or on a boat.

2. Pretend you were building a beach house. How would you have it built? Ask questions, such as: "Would it be one level or have an upstairs?" "How many bedrooms would it have?" "What would the front door look like?" "Would it have large or small windows?"

3. What would be fun about living at the beach? The beach is within walking distance. You can sleep to the sounds of the ocean. It would be easy to collect shells.

4. What are things you might not like, if you lived at the beach? Sand might easily get inside your house. It might be foggy or more chilly when the sun is not out. A storm with large waves could wash water into your house or knock it down.

Materials:

Small wooden or colored blocks, tin foil, pipe cleaners, small rocks, colored construction paper, scissors, posterboard.

Preparation:

Cut the paper and tin foil into squares. Make at least two squares for each child. Cut a square of posterboard, at least twice as wide. Make one for each child.

Things to do:

1. Sit in a circle. Place the above materials on the rug.

2. Give everyone a posterboard square. This is the foundation for your beach house.

3. Pass out the collected material. Each child can receive a certain number of blocks, pipe cleaners, rocks, paper squares and tin foil.

4. Design your beach house. The paper squares can be rugs, halls or carpet. The tin foil can be folded into roofs or furniture.

5. When everyone has finished building their beach house, display the houses. Form a beach town. Think of a name for your beach town. Make a sign that welcomes visitors.

More Ideas:

• Put a "For Sale," sign by each house. Place play money by the beach houses. Parents can buy the beach houses. When a beach house is purchased, place a sold sign by the house.

One Little Fish

Things to talk about:

1. Ask the question: "What do fish eat in the ocean?" Brainstorm! They eat very small sea animals called plankton; They eat plants; They eat sea creatures, such as, sea snails, crabs, and animals inside shells. They eat other fish.
2. If you were a small fish, would you eat a bigger fish or a fish smaller then you?
3. If you were a very big fish, what would you be afraid of? A bigger fish.
4. This is called a food chain. Make two fists and place them in front of you. These are two fish. Take one of your fists and open it. Place it over your other fist, so it covers it. Now say: The bigger fish eats the smaller fish.
5. Repeat this action, back and forth, each hand covering the other fist. As you do this, over and over, say the following words: The bigger eats the smaller.
6. After you do this, at least four times, spread out your arms and say: And the biggest fish eats everybody.

Materials: None

Preparation: None

Things to do:

1. Say the following finger play. Place one hand behind you. The fingers on this hand are the fishes. They will swim out in front of you, matching the number of fishes in each verse. Make them wiggle.
2. Your other hand is the shark. Make swimming movements with your shark hand. Move slowly. When your shark eats the fish, open your hand and grab the wiggling fishes.
3. When you say the word burrrrrrp, slowly open your shark hand. Then wiggle all five fingers on your fish hand and make them swim behind you.

One little fish swam out to sea,
Where oh where is my family?
Along came a shark and quiet as could be,
Ate that fish in the deep blue sea!

Two little fishes swam out to sea,
Where oh where is my family?
Along came a shark and quiet as could be,
Ate those fishes in the deep blue sea!

Three little fishes swam out to sea,
Where oh where is my family?
Along came a shark and quiet as could be,
Ate those fishes in the deep blue sea!

Four little fishes swam out to sea,
Where oh where is my family?
Along came a shark and quiet as could be,
Ate those fishes in the deep blue sea!

Five little fishes swam out to sea,
Where oh where is my family?
Along came a shark and quiet as could be,
Ate those fishes in the deep blue sea!

Burrrrrrp!
Out swam the fishes and hid behind me!

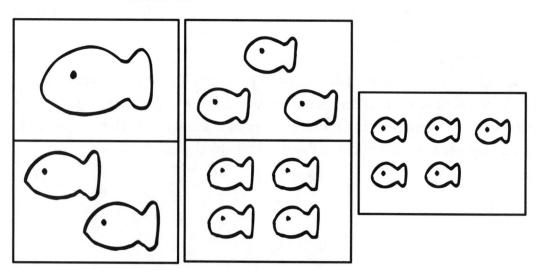

More Ideas:

• Sing this song often. Change the word fish to different sea animals.

Sea Monster Hunt!

Things to talk about:

1. Name sea creatures that live in the ocean. Think of as many as you can.
2. Creatures that you have named live near the top and middle of the ocean. There are sea creatures that live near the very bottom. Do you think it is dark or light near the bottom of the ocean? It is dark. The sun's rays do not reach the bottom of the ocean.
3. Very strange and scary looking fish live near the very bottom. Brainstorm what these fish might look like. Possible ideas might be: Large eyes; big mouths; strange shapes; large teeth; gigantic jaws; and weird patterns.
4. Some people claim to have seen sea monsters. Do you think there might be sea monsters in the ocean?
5. What do you think a sea monster would look like? What would he sound like? What would he eat?

Materials: None

Preparation: None

Things to talk about:

Go on a Sea Monster Hunt. Say this chant to the tune of *I'm Going on a Bear Hunt!* Slap your thighs back and forth as you say, I'm going to find a sea monster. Then do the suggested movements. Make your movements slow and suspenseful.

Slap your things for a running movement!
Push through the seaweed forest!
Run along the sandy bottom!
Grab onto the giant eel!
Dive upward!
Swim back to shore!
Place arms over your head and hide inside
A giant clam!

I'm going to find a sea monster. I'm going to find a sea monster. Let's swim across the ocean! (*Pretend to swim.*)

I'm going to find a sea monster. I'm going to find a sea monster. Let's dive down! (*Place palms together and move them back and forth.*)

I'm going to find a sea monster. I'm going to find a sea monster. Grab onto a giant eel! (*Holds hands together, arms straight and weave back and forth.*)

I'm going to find a sea monster. I'm going to find a sea monster. Walk along the sandy bottom! (*Slap your hands on the rug.*)

I'm going to find a sea monster. I'm going to find a sea monster. Move through the seaweed forest! (*Push back and forth with your hands.*)

I'm going on a sea monster hunt. I'm going on a sea monster hunt. I see a sea cave. Let's tiptoe in! (*Slowly walk with your fingers on the rug.*)

Do you see anything big and scary? (*Place a hand over the top of an eye.*)
Not yet!

Take out your flashlights. (*Unhook them from your belt and shine them around.*)
Aaaaaaah! I see a sea monster! Run!

More Ideas:

• Lower the lights. Draw a sea monster and tape it on a wall near the children. When you see the sea monster in the cave, have a real flashlight that you shine on the sea monster.